What Every Teacher
Should Know About
Media and Technology

What Every Teacher Should Know About...

What Every Teacher Should Know About
Diverse Learners

What Every Teacher Should Know About
Student Motivation

What Every Teacher Should Know About
Learning, Memory, and the Brain

What Every Teacher Should Know About
Instructional Planning

What Every Teacher Should Know About
Effective Teaching Strategies

What Every Teacher Should Know About
Classroom Management and Discipline

What Every Teacher Should Know About
Student Assessment

What Every Teacher Should Know About
Special Learners

What Every Teacher Should Know About
Media and Technology

What Every Teacher Should Know About
The Profession and Politics of Teaching

DONNA WALKER TILESTON

What Every Teacher Should Know About
Media and Technology

CORWIN PRESS
A Sage Publications Company
Thousand Oaks, California

For information:

Corwin Press
A Sage Publications Company
2455 Teller Road
Thousand Oaks, California 91320
www.corwinpress.com

Sage Publications Ltd.
6 Bonhill Street
London EC2A 4PU
United Kingdom

Sage Publications India Pvt. Ltd.
B-42, Panchsheel Enclave
Post Box 4109
New Delhi 110 017 India

Printed in the United States of America

Library of Congress Cataloging-in-Publication Data

Tileston, Donna Walker.
What every teacher should know about media and technology /
Donna Walker Tileston.
    p. cm. — (What every teacher should know about—; 9)
Includes bibliographical references and index.
ISBN 0-7619-3125-2 (Paper)
    1. Educational technology—Handbooks, manuals, etc. 2. Media literacy—Handbooks, manuals, etc. 3. Internet in education—Handbooks, manuals, etc. I. Title. II. Series.
LB1028.3.T59 2004
371.33—dc21   2003013401

This book is printed on acid-free paper.

06   10   9   8   7   6   5   4

Acquisitions Editor:	Faye Zucker
Editorial Assistant:	Stacy Wagner
Production Editor:	Diane S. Foster
Copy Editor:	Stacey Shimizu
Typesetter:	C&M Digitals (P) Ltd.
Proofreader:	Mary Meagher
Indexer:	Molly Hall
Cover Designer:	Tracy E. Miller
Production Artist:	Lisa Miller

Contents

About the Author   vii

Acknowledgments   ix

Introduction   xi

Vocabulary Pre-Test   xii

1. **The Importance of Media in the Classroom**   **1**
    Why Media Is Brain Friendly   2
    The Effect of Media on Student Modalities   3
    The Effect of Media on Motivation   3
    The Effect of Media on Behavior Management   4
    The Effect of Media on Reaching Higher
        Levels of Thought   5
    The Effect of Media on Real-World Applications   6

2. **Using Media to Plan and Introduce a Lesson**   **9**
    Begin With Goals for the Learning   11
    Build Declarative Objectives   12
    Develop Procedural Objectives   18
    Provide a Matrix or Rubric   20

3. **Using Media for Teaching**   **23**
    The Basics   23
    Using Technology to Teach Standards   27
    Higher-Level Thinking Skills   33

4. **Using Media to Enhance Student Products**   **39**
    Making Choices on Products   40
    Following a Guide for Research   46

5. Viewing the Big Picture: Keeping Up 51
  Being an Agent of Change 54
  Creating a Plan for the Classroom 54
  Technology = Success 55

Vocabulary Summary 57

Vocabulary Post-Test 63

References 69

Index 71

About the Author

Donna Walker Tileston, Ed.D., is a veteran teacher of 27 years and the president of Strategic Teaching and Learning, a consulting firm that provides services to schools throughout the United States and Canada. Also an author, Donna's publications include *Strategies for Teaching Differently: On the Block or Not* (Corwin Press, 1998), *Innovative Strategies of the Block Schedule* (Bureau of Education and Research [BER], 1999), and *Ten Best Teaching Practices: How Brain Research, Learning Styles, and Standards Define Teaching Competencies* (Corwin Press, 2000), which has been on Corwin's best-seller list since its first year in print.

Donna received her B.A. from the University of North Texas, her M.A. from East Texas State University, and her Ed.D. from Texas A & M University-Commerce. She may be reached at www.strategicteachinglearning.com or by e-mail at dwtileston@yahoo.com.

To my grandson and the joy of my life, Joshua Walker McBrayer.
May you have every opportunity to excel in this multimedia world.

Acknowledgments

My sincere thanks go to my Acquisitions Editor, Faye Zucker, for her faith in education and what this information can do to help all children be successful. Without Faye, these books would not have been possible.

I had the best team of editors around: Diane Foster, Stacy Wagner, and Stacey Shimizu. You took my words and you gave them power. Thank you.

Thanks to my wonderful Board Chairman at Strategic Teaching and Learning, Dulany Howland: Thank you for sticking with me in the good times and the tough spots. Your expertise and friendship have been invaluable.

Introduction

Throughout my books, I have discussed the issues important to helping all students be successful. We know that the majority of students in any given classroom are either visual or kinesthetic learners; they need to see and experience the learning before it makes sense personally. That is an important point, because we learn and remember best those things that make sense to us. If you have ever tried to memorize data that made no sense to you, you know what I mean.

I have included this book on using media in the *What Every Teacher Should Know . . .* series of books, because I believe that when we add a variety of media into the classroom, we significantly raise the possibility that we will reach all students. My goal is not to provide a book on the future of computer use but rather to discuss what is relevant now. In this book, I will discuss how the use of computers and other media can help us meet standards, provide better and more exciting lessons, and assess more thoroughly. I begin where we should begin in the classroom—with the vocabulary of the book.

Write your definition of the words as they relate to media in Form 0.1. After reading this book, revisit what you have written to see if you want to expand or change your original definition.

This book also includes a pre-test on the vocabulary used throughout this book. The Vocabulary Summary at the end of the book contains the terms and their definitions. Once you have finished the book, you will be given a second chance to show what you know on a vocabulary post-test.

Form 0.1   Vocabulary List for Media and Technology

Vocabulary Word	Your Definition	Final Definition
Bloom's Taxonomy		
Channel One		
Classroom climate		
Classroom management		
Cognitive development		
Computer-assisted instruction		
Creative and productive thinking		
Critical thinking		
Cyber schools		
Direct instruction		
Discovery learning		
Distance learning		
Higher-order thinking		
Linguistic organizers		
Multimedia		
Nonlinguistic organizers		
Primary sources		
Problem-based learning		
Rubric		
Scaffolding		
Secondary sources		
Student products		

Vocabulary
Pre-Test

Instructions: For each question given, choose the best answer. Only one answer is correct.

1. Critics of technology use in schools have as their *main* concern . . .
   A. The research results on the use of technology in schools
   B. The inappropriate use of the Internet
   C. The appropriateness of the computer to the lessons
   D. The use of the computers by students to e-mail each other

2. In a classroom in which students are provided information in a step-by-step format, we say the students are being taught by . . .
   A. Discovery learning
   B. Problem-based learning
   C. Scaffolding
   D. Direct instruction

3. Students who rely on the Internet for research are primarily using what?
   A. Secondary sources
   B. Scaffolding
   C. Primary sources
   D. Problem-based learning

4. Marty Perez's language arts and social studies classes were given a newspaper article about a company that wants to relocate to a Latin American country. Ms. Perez has asked her students to work in small groups as they research and put together a proposal to sell the company on the country they have chosen. This type of teaching technique is called . . .
   A. Scaffolding
   B. Problem-based learning
   C. Primary sources
   D. Direct instruction

5. In Jim Brown's mathematics class, he uses music, PowerPoint, and discussion for teaching. What technique is Mr. Brown using?
   A. Problem-based learning
   B. Direct instruction
   C. Discovery learning
   D. Multimedia

6. Shonda Marshall is starting a unit on the Vietnam War. She has placed her students in small groups and given them a packet that contains maps of the area as it was at the time of the war, maps of the area as it is now, names of major battles, and the names of key players. Ms. Marshall took her class to the computer lab for a scavenger hunt to find the information required in her packet. What technique is Ms. Marshall using?
   A. Distance learning
   B. Discovery learning
   C. Primary sources
   D. Linguistic organizers

7. Which of the following statements is *not* true?
   A. Rubrics should be given to students prior to the learning.
   B. Rubrics show levels of understanding.
   C. Tutorials for rubrics are available on the Internet.
   D. Rubrics should not be used as an assessment for a unit of study.

8. Martina is a middle school student. Her teacher provides the students with a great deal of direct instruction and feedback at the beginning of a unit and then gradually puts the students into opportunities to learn on their own. Martina's teacher is practicing . . .
   A. Computer-assisted instruction
   B. Creative and productive thinking
   C. Scaffolding
   D. Problem-based learning

9. Students at Blair Elementary are working on a project that requires them to use forensic evidence to explain a given problem. Which of the following are the students *not* practicing?
   A. Problem-based learning
   B. Higher-order thinking
   C. Critical thinking
   D. Computer-assisted instruction

10. Nicole is taking a class on speech pathology on the Internet. This is an example of . . .
    A. Computer-assisted instruction
    B. Problem-based learning
    C. Distance learning
    D. Discovery learning

11. Which of the following would *not* be an example of a linguistic organizer?
    A. A mind map
    B. An outline
    C. A learning log
    D. A chart for math formulas

12. Which of the following would *not* be an example of a nonlinguistic organizer?
    A. A mind map
    B. A learning log
    C. A sequence organizer
    D. A fishbone

13. Using television as a media source sometimes draws criticism because . . .
    A. It is commercialized
    B. It takes up too much time
    C. It has questionable value
    D. It is too low tech

14. The modality most often found in school is . . .
    A. Multimodal
    B. Auditory
    C. Visual
    D. Kinesthetic

15. Students in Mr. Brown's class are using a Website that shows them the original Declaration of Independence. They are using . . .
    A. An expensive program
    B. Secondary sources
    C. Multimedia programming
    D. Primary sources

16. When teachers use the project method of teaching, they should remember that . . . (Which is *not* true?)
    A. They need procedural objectives
    B. They need examples from each modality
    C. Students do not need a lot of direction
    D. Students do need a lot of feedback

17. Kenny presented his report using PowerPoint®. This is an example of . . .
    A. A visual product
    B. A kinesthetic product
    C. An auditory product
    D. A nonlinguistic product

18. Drew presented his report as a dialogue typed on the computer and read to the class. This is an example of . . .
    A. A visual product
    B. A kinesthetic product

C. An auditory product

D. A nonlinguistic product

19. Shelly presented her report as a model drawn on the computer accompanied by sound and motion. Her report is an example of . . .

A. Multimedia

B. A linguistic product

C. Secondary sources

D. Cyber schools

20. Margot created a computer game to help her fellow students learn math facts. This is an example of . . .

A. Analysis

B. Synthesis

C. Evaluation

D. Distance learning

1

The Importance of Media in the Classroom

A s teachers, we have a wealth of information from which to choose for our classrooms. We can now bring history into the classroom through pictures, music, and other visuals to a degree never before possible. We can communicate with students from other countries, and we can take classes from teachers we have never met in places we have never been. We can apply the physics from the classroom to simulations available to us through the Internet, and we can develop projects across grade levels and campuses. Students are no longer limited by the walls of a classroom or the knowledge of a single textbook. The world is available to most classrooms, even when students do not have their own computers.

We can bring the media into the classroom through visuals, sounds, smells, and tastes. Because our brains rely heavily on stimulus from the outside for learning, this is just one of the reasons that teaching with media is brain friendly. In addition, we should bring technology to the classroom because:

- Technology is not limited by the classroom walls.
- Technology does not know or care what the student's socioeconomic status may be, and thus helps to level the playing field for these students.
- Technology provides an equal opportunity for everyone to learn.
- Technology is more in tune with the way our students learn today.
- Technology is so much a part of the real world that to limit its use in the classroom is to limit our students' ability to compete in the world.

WHY MEDIA IS BRAIN FRIENDLY

Most researchers define *brain-compatible learning* as learning that occurs:

- Using modalities that are most comfortable for the learner. For example, most learners are either visual or kinesthetic, thus a brain-friendly environment will lean heavily on teaching methods that include visuals, models, or hands-on activities.
- In an environment that is positive and friendly and incorporates high expectations for everyone.
- In a classroom that utilizes research-based methods for teaching and learning.
- In a classroom that provides a variety of opportunities for learning.
- In a classroom that is flexible in terms of time, resources, and structures. For example, if something is not working, the problem is identified, diagnosed, and fixed rather than just moving on. If students need more time to learn, more time is given rather than sticking to a fixed timetable, regardless of the quality of the learning.
- In a classroom where quality is important and students are given rubrics or matrices that tell them in advance what is expected.

- In a classroom where standards are used and where students know the expectations. The students are provided opportunities to review their work in terms of given standards so that they know at all times where they stand.
- When specific feedback is given consistently and frequently. Just saying "Good job" is not enough.

We are being encouraged to use brain-based strategies in our classrooms; one of the best ways to do so is through the use of media in the teaching/learning processes. In this chapter, we will examine several ways that using media enhances the principles of brain-based learning.

THE EFFECT OF MEDIA ON STUDENT MODALITIES

As I have discussed in most of my books, about 98% of all incoming information to the brain comes through the senses. Add to that the fact that over 87% of the learners in the classroom prefer to learn by visual and tactile means, and you have a recipe for failure if the primary methods of teaching are auditory. In *Growing Up Digital* (1998), Don Tapscott said that this "Net Generation" watches much less television than did its parents. The television is not interactive, and this generation prefers to be active participants in all that they do. Tapscott cited a 1997 survey by Teenage Research Unlimited, in which 80% of the teenagers polled said it is "in" to be online—right up there with dating and partying.

THE EFFECT OF MEDIA ON MOTIVATION

According to Jensen (1997), interactive abstract learning that includes the use of various media, such as CD-ROMs, the Internet, distance learning, or virtual reality, utilizes the categorical memory and requires little intrinsic motivation. Although traditional forms of education receive the greatest amount of the education dollars, they require a great deal of intrinsic motivation to be effective. Students must struggle to make the traditional type of learning work, since it is outside the context of its meaning.

In addition, students from inner-city poverty learn in context—usually from stories—and to require them to learn all day in an environment that is not brain friendly for them helps to set them up for failure. Similarly, English language learners need visual stimulus to help them to process and store the information that comes from words. They often do not have the language acquisition skills in English to store a great deal of dialogue in a way that can be easily retrieved when needed. Semantic information (i.e., words, facts, and names) is stored in the semantic memory system—the least effective of the memory systems of the brain.

In order to have meaning to the learner in terms of retrieval, semantic information must have a connector. Try memorizing a long list of words and you will see what I mean. The brain was not created for memorizing meaningless information. If you try to memorize a long list of words, you will probably find yourself devising a plan to help you, such as creating acronyms or developing a story around the words to help you memorize them. You are giving the words a context or connection to help you remember. Contextual learning is stored in the episodic memory system, which is much better at remembering. Remember, the next time you require students to learn a list of items, that the more context you can provide, the stronger the recall. Using media in the form of auditory or visual stimulus can help you do this.

THE EFFECT OF MEDIA ON BEHAVIOR MANAGEMENT

If you have read *What Every Teacher Should Know About Classroom Management and Discipline* (Tileston, 2004a), you know that most of the discipline problems in the classroom are caused by such factors as boredom, not understanding the relevance of the information, and incorrect modalities for learning. You also know that over 87% of the students in any given classroom are visual learners.

Students who enter our classrooms have been a part of a multimedia world since birth. Students today were able to insert videos or DVDs of children's programs into the appropriate devices for viewing from the time that they were three years old. If they want to know something, they search the Internet. It should not be surprising to us that these same students have difficulty sitting all day in classrooms that rely on low technology, such as overheads, whiteboards, lectures, and note taking, as the major sources of information gathering. For the majority of students, who are visual, just hearing the information is not enough; they need to see it and to experience it. We lament the fact that students do so poorly in mathematics and yet we teach this subject primarily by lecture and homework (i.e., drill and practice). If we can find ways to help these students see how the math works and how it is applied to the real world, we are more likely to have better math students. Media can help us get there quickly.

THE EFFECT OF MEDIA ON
REACHING HIGHER LEVELS OF THOUGHT

There are so many great Websites that encourage and teach higher-level thinking that we do an injustice to our students if we do not lead them there. Using media is the key to moving students to higher-level thinking. Our students are already familiar with using the Internet and many of the software programs required to reach such higher-level thinking skills as creativity, problem solving, comparison and contrast, and evaluation. We need to lead them to the best of the best in term of media and to provide feedback as they work. Real-world applications, such as the physics software that explores how to design amusement park rides utilizing g-forces without damaging the body, are exciting and fun, but they also lead students into problem solving and decision making.

In a study by Harold Wenglinsky (1998) on the impact of media on learning mathematics among fourth and eighth graders, it was concluded that when computers are used to perform tasks applying higher-order concepts and when teachers are proficient in directing students toward productive uses, computers are associated with significant learning gains.

The Effect of Media on Real-World Applications

We know that motivation to learn and to complete tasks is directly related to the student's perception of the relevance of the learning. All learning seems to begin in the self-system of the brain. This is the system that decides whether or not to engage in the learning. "If the task is judged important, if the probability of success is high, and a positive affect is generated or associated with the task, the individual will be motivated to engage in the new task" (Marzano, Pickering, & Pollock, 2001).

In *What Every Teacher Should Know About Learning, Memory, and the Brain* (Tileston, 2004c), I note that one critical question asked by the brain in determining to what to pay attention to is whether the information is important: Information can be important to the teacher and to the students, but unless the student believes the information is important, the self-system will not view it as important.

As teachers, we must not only let our students know the importance of the learning but also how it will be important to our students personally. Marzano, Pickering, and Pollock (2001) explain it this way, "What an individual considers to be important is probably a function of the extent to which it meets one of two conditions: it is perceived as instrumental in satisfying a basic need, or it is perceived as instrumental in the attainment of a personal goal." In working with students from poverty or from the inner city, this is an especially important aspect of the learning. Probably telling these students that the learning is important because they will need it for college is not going to provide motivation to learn.

While teachers can and do provide real-world applications to the learning in other ways, the use of media is a great tool to lead students to real-world examples. Three examples of how teachers have effectively tied classroom information to real-world experiences can be found at www.netc.org/classrooms@work. At this wonderful site, three educators—elementary, middle, and high school teachers—provide insight into how they make real-world connections in their units. At the elementary level, teacher Jane Krauss created a 15-week thematic geography unit for her fourth and fifth graders called *Travel USA*. Using geography, history, science, and language arts skills, students take a German family on a tour of the United States. Students used the Internet to research information for their project. Ms. Krauss created a travel Website for the students as a guide.

Middle school teachers Theresa Maves, Meile Harris, and Jill Whitesell combined science, mathematics, and language arts for their eight-week project to design and develop an amusement park ride that safely uses g-forces. Their project, called *It's a Wild Ride,* includes the use of computer-based motion detectors and graphing software.

High school students in Peter Knowles' class were challenged to find a new production facility in Latin America for the company Mega Opus International (OPI). This producer of small personal appliances, high-tech entertainment devices, automobiles, apparel, and electromagnetic transportation systems offered the host country many benefits including jobs and a higher standard of living. Students researched and presented bids on behalf of their countries for the project. Computers were used not only for the research but also to create the charts, graphs, and spreadsheets within their bid packages.

These projects represent a much more exciting and effective way to learn than simply reading and taking notes, followed by a test on Friday.

2

Using Media to Plan and Introduce a Lesson

Media is not just for use in student projects; using media can help make a teacher's job easier and more exciting. From help in planning the lesson to ideas for assessments, there are many interesting resources available through various media today. Website addresses (URLs) change frequently. If you can't find a given site, try searching for it by name or key word at a search engine like Google or Yahoo.

At www.teachnet.com teachers can download an Excel worksheet to keep up with lesson plans or get an idea about how to do their own lesson plans using a spreadsheet. This Website also contains ideas for bulletin boards and for lessons. Are you a new teacher? A great ebsite to help you in your planning is www.new-teacher.com.

If you start the day with a thought puzzle or question, as I do while I am checking role, you might try one of the following sites.

For questions about current events:

- ABC (www.abc.abcnews.go.com)
- CBS (www.cbs.com)
- CNN (www.cnn.com)
- NBC (www.nbc.com)
- Time for Kids (www.timeforkids.com)
- USA Today (www.usatoday.com)
- The Washington Post (www.washingtonpost.com)
- The Weather Channel (www.weather.com)

For historical events:

- Franklin Institute (www.fi.edu), which includes events in history, math, science, and literature
- This day in history (www.historychannel.com/thisday)

For science:

- The astronomy photo of the day (www.antwrp.gsfc. nasa.gov/apod/astropix.html)

For music:

- The Garden State Pops Youth Orchestra's "This day in music history" (www.gspyo.com)

For art:

- Art links (www.dart.fine-art.com/artlinks), which includes links to artists, galleries and exhibits and museums

For language arts:

- The Flat Stanley Website (flatstanley.enoreo.on.ca/)

I like to start my day with Mindjogs, described in *Ten Best Teaching Practices* (Tileston, 2000). Mindjogs are thought questions and puzzles designed to get the oxygen up in the brain and prepare the students for the learning. They also accomplish another goal: getting students into their seats and working while I check roll and do those other teacher's tasks at the beginning of class. My students love them—even my college students.

Some Websites that are good sources for Mindjogs include www.skinema.com and www.tomvolkfungi.net. At the latter site, University of Wisconsin professor Tom Volk provides a fungus of the month for his college students: They must give its common and proper names. He does some really funny things for holidays, like providing all the fungi that can attack the Thanksgiving dinner. Skinema.com features skin diseases of the rich and famous along with music, video, and audio. Want to put your Mindjogs on the Internet but not sure how? Www.webmonkey.com will help you design your own Web page. If your school does not have a server on which you can place your Web page, go to Teacher Tools, My School Online at www.teachervision.com for a Website that will host your page.

Once you introduce your students to the world of Mindjogs, provide opportunities for them to come up with starters for the day. Even our first graders can do this with the aid of PowerPoint, word-processing programs, and music.

Now, let's look at the steps to good planning and how media can help the classroom teacher in this task. In *What Every Teacher Should Know About Instructional Planning* (Tileston, 2004b), I provide the steps for good planning. Figure 2.1, adapted from that volume, is a graphic model of those steps.

Begin With Goals for the Learning

Use the state goals as a guide in deciding what to teach. State goals and standards are available on the Internet. If you do not know the address for your state, you can run a search on any of the search engines, such as Google, by typing in your state name and education agency or department. A Website that provides the doorway into all states is www.statestandards.com, where state goals for each state can be found along with other information, such as sample tests and information about the assessment

Figure 2.1   Planning Steps

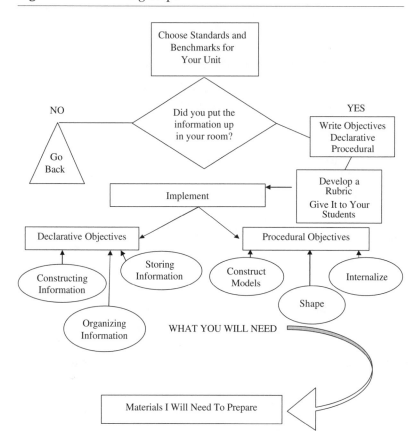

tests. Use the table tool on your word-processing software to list the goals for the lesson.

BUILD DECLARATIVE OBJECTIVES

Develop declarative objectives for the learning based on the state standards and benchmarks. Declarative objectives cover the factual knowledge that we want our students to know as a result of the learning and have three purposes: to help students construct information, organize it, and store it. Figure 2.2 is a graphic model of declarative objectives. Let's

Figure 2.2   Working With Declarative Objectives

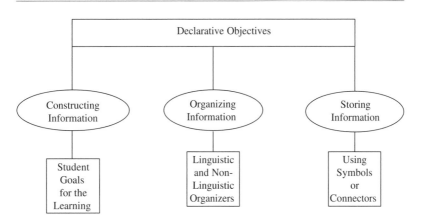

look at each of these purposes and how using media will help students to reach those goals.

Helping Students Construct Meaning

We help students to construct meaning from the learning by doing the following things.

Asking students to provide their own goals for the learning. Building a matrix can help students to create their own learning goals. Table 2.1 is an example of a matrix that students might use to build their goals. This is an important step, because the self-system and metacognitive systems of the brain, which control motivation and impulsivity, rely on goals set by the individual. If you want your students to be motivated to start a process and complete it with high energy, teach them how to set goals, monitor them, and change them as needed during the process.

Helping students make connections. One of the most important things that we do at the beginning of a new unit or body of knowledge is to help students make connections between what they already know or have experienced and the new

Table 2.1   Learning Goals

State your local goal	State your learning goal	How will you meet your goal?	Was your goal met? If not, why not?
Students will learn geometric shapes.	I will learn how to make each shape and where I can find them in the classroom and school.	I will make a shape book that contains each of the shapes and examples of the shapes. I will go on a scavenger hunt with my class to find shapes.	

knowledge that they are about to undertake. This process is defined as "Linking old knowledge with new knowledge, making predictions, verifying them and filling in a lot of unstated information" (Marzano, 2000).

Visuals, such as pictures, graphs, and computer-generated research, can be used to do this. Music is also helpful in assisting students to make connections to the new information. I like to bring in sounds and pictures to begin a unit. Time Life is a great source for CDs and pictures of events in history as they really happened. For example, the book *We Interrupt This Broadcast* (Garner, 1998) has pictures and recordings of events in history as they were happening. It is the next best thing to being there.

Providing advance thinking about the unit. Send students on a scavenger hunt through the Internet to find pieces of information that will be utilized within the unit of study. By doing this, you are providing interest and anticipation to the information. Use the Time Life series or pictures and sounds from Websites, such as www.pbs.org, to spark interest in your students and to build curiosity about the unit.

If you are in a school with distance-learning capabilities or video conferencing, which allow you to go virtually to another location, take your students to the zoo or to a wonderful museum virtually. If your school does not have one of these labs, take your students on a field trip to a nearby university or college that has this capability. The first time that we took our first graders to the San Diego zoo virtually, they were initially a little in awe of the docent and the technology, but it was not long until they were communicating with the zoo staff as if they were actually physically there.

You might plan an interdisciplinary unit around Dr. Seuss's book *Oh, the Places You'll Go* and take your students on a virtual trip as a culminating activity. In physics, as we studied g-forces and their effects over time on amusement rides, the students first visited amusement parks virtually and then in actuality after designing their own amusement rides, showing the g-force and the effects on the body at each point in the ride.

Introducing a new unit with music. Begin a new unit by creating the "sounds of the time" through music. For example, for a unit on World War II, bring in music from that era to introduce the topic. Songs of the time include such tunes as "Boogie-Woogie Bugle Boy." Ask students to search the Internet for the meaning to *boogie-woogie* for that time.

Introducing a new unit with pictures. Start a new unit by showing pictures from the Internet. For example, I begin a unit on the study of natural disasters with a picture from the Internet showing the aftermath of the most disastrous earthquake in California history. When I read to first graders, I make a PowerPoint presentation using some of the pages from the book we are reading. Since most students are visual, it is important that all students can see the pictures from the book. A good Website for introducing your students to meaningful use of the Internet for research is www.newsbank.com, a site that not only guides students through how to research, but provides sample of original documents as well.

Helping Students
Organize Declarative Knowledge

The second phase of teaching declarative knowledge is helping students to organize the new information. The more we can put information into visual representations, the more we will help our students to construct meaning and to put the information into long-term memory. Jensen (1997) says that at least 87% of the students in the classroom are visual learners; this means that they must see the learning to construct meaning. Visual organizers, sometimes called nonlinguistic organizers, graphic organizers, or advance organizers, help the brain to organize and make patterns of the information studied. The Website, www.engine-uity.com, is one I love to use for project ideas. If you teach secondary students, do not be put off by the logo for this site (a cartoon train): This site has very high-level materials for all grade levels. At the high school level, check out the "Rats Packs."

Graphic organizers are one of the best ways to help students put information into manageable chunks and to provide a pattern. Since the brain is a pattern-seeking organ, this one strategy has enormous potential for raising the learning level of students. A great Website to introduce you to the teaching and drawing of graphic organizers is www.thinking maps.com. This site will introduce you to basic maps and when they should be used. For example, it suggests that teachers use the following:

- Circles maps for defining something in context
- Tree maps for classifying and grouping
- Bubble maps for describing using adjectives
- Double bubble maps for comparing and contrasting
- Flow maps for sequencing and ordering information
- Brace maps for identifying part/whole relationships
- Bridge maps for seeing analogies

Software is available for developing these maps or you can make your own using basic computer tools and auto shapes.

Help Students Store Declarative Information

The third step for teachers is helping students to store declarative information.

I have said that declarative knowledge is the most difficult kind of knowledge for the brain to store, particularly if it is taught in the traditional method of lecture with drill and practice. There are, however, some tools that can help the brain to store the information in a more acceptable way. Some of those tools are as follows:

- Use symbols to help the brain put the information into categories or patterns. For example, if you are teaching a class that requires a great deal of vocabulary, create symbols to put at the top of each sheet to help the students (and their brains) sort the information. Use the symbols from autoshapes function of your word-processing or drawing program, download pictures from the Internet, or make your own with drawing tools or software programs such as PrintShop.

- When making graphic organizers, teach students to use symbols as well as words. This will help them to store the information more efficiently and to have better recall. Students, too, may download images from the Internet or create their own using common computer software programs.

- You need not spend a great deal of time drawing graphic organizers to show your students the process. The Web is full of great sites for making organizers quickly and easily. Two that I often use are www.thinkingmaps.com and www.inspiration.com.

- For vocabulary words, ask students to provide a symbol for each word to help them remember it. You can create a table using the table tool of your word-processing program, and then students can either draw symbols or download them from the Internet.

- Use visual tools, such as the nonlinguistic organizers provided on the www.thinkingmaps.com Website.

Figure 2.3   Working With Procedural Objectives

```
┌─────────────────────────────────────────────────────┐
│                 Procedural Objectives                │
└─────────────────────────────────────────────────────┘
         │                    │                  │
   ╭───────────╮        ╭───────────╮      ╭───────────╮
   │ Construct │        │   Shape   │      │ Internalize│
   │  Models   │        │           │      │           │
   ╰───────────╯        ╰───────────╯      ╰───────────╯

      Mental          Make the Model        Perform
       and              My Own         Until Internalized
      Actual
```

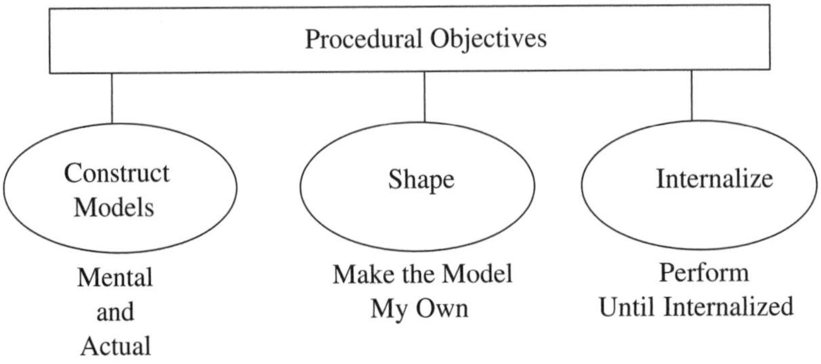

DEVELOP PROCEDURAL OBJECTIVES

Procedural objectives are those objectives built around what we want students to be able to do (i.e., to demonstrate through written, oral, kinesthetic, or other means). They show what students can do with the declarative information. We teach declarative information first, because students need to know the vocabulary, facts, people, and such before performing a procedure.

There are three phases to procedural knowledge: constructing models in the mind, shaping the information, and internalizing the process to the point that it is automatic (sometimes called *automaticity*). Figure 2.3 is a graphic organizer showing the parts to procedural objectives. We can use media and technology to help students accomplish these three steps by sending them to Websites for specific pictures on the learning, by taking them on a virtual field trip through the use of a virtual learning lab, by using graphic organizers, and by allowing them to practice skills using the computer instead of paper and pencil only.

Constructing Models

First, students need to be able to construct models of the learning mentally and, in some cases, actually. This might be accomplished through imagery, through graphic models, or through student projects. Students use declarative information to construct the model or project—to decide what it will look like, feel like, and so forth. It is difficult to make a basket in basketball if you have never mentally imagined doing that: The same is true with procedural activities. Help students to visualize doing an activity and doing it well.

Use technology to help them plan and design their final product by sending students to Websites that offer examples of good models. Provide many visuals on the topics studied to help students with their mental models. Through software, students may be able to construct their model completely on the computer. For example, students who are designing a newspaper layout, brochure, or flyer for their project may want to use one of the presentation programs or a software suite, such as AppleWorks or Microsoft Works.

Students who want to create PowerPoint presentations for their projects may want to go beyond the typical graphics that come with this program by going to the graphics online tool in PowerPoint. Sound, pictures, and animation are easily added to these presentations. If students want to record their own voices onto the presentation, this can be done with an inexpensive microphone attached to the computer. To view ideas for exciting presentations, take your students to www.presentationpro.com and download the free trial software. This site changes often and has great ideas for making better use of graphics and sound.

Shaping Information

Second, students need to be able to shape the information so that it becomes their own. Some of the ways that we help students shape the new information is by providing opportunities to practice the learning and by giving them clues about how to make the process work smoothly. For example, in the unit on building models of amusement park rides, students were given opportunities to examine various rides and to visualize first what they would do with their own rides. They were given software to design and test their ideas many times before actually presenting them. By using software, they were able to make changes as needed throughout the process. Graphic organizers and models for brochures, flyers, and so forth are also a great way to help students shape the information into their own product.

Internalizing Information

We help students internalize and give the information automaticity by providing adequate opportunities for them to work with the process and by providing feedback often. Students need the time to practice an activity until it becomes automatic for them. If we did not practice math or if students had not been allowed to practice with their park rides designs, the results would not be of high quality. Students need both massed practice (also know as *immersion*) and practice over time before the process becomes internalized. Immersion is a great tool, but if we do not come back to the learning from time to time, often the learning is lost. That is why students may do well on the test this Friday over the math concepts studied this week, but try giving them a problem from this week's work three weeks from now.

To the extent possible, provide opportunities for students to practice the learning on the computer instead of with paper and pencil. Make homework more meaningful by assigning activities that are not rote and that are original instead of more of the same from the classroom. For example, ask students to make a mind map of the major points discussed in class or of pages from the text. You might say, "Read pages 87 to 95 in your text tonight and mind map the key points that the authors are making." This type of homework is much more meaningful, and it is more difficult to copy someone else's homework.

PROVIDE A MATRIX OR RUBRIC

If we want consistently to receive quality products from our students, we must tell them up front what we mean by quality.

Table 2.2   Rubric Made Using a Table Tool

Expert	Emerging	Beginning	Not Yet
Student understands the information and is able to write and say what he/she knows in his/her own words.	Student demonstrates some understanding and can say or write the information with some help.	Student show a minimum understanding and can explain with cues and coaching from teacher.	Student can repeat information, but shows no ability to understand what is being said.

Table 2.3   Matrix Made Using a Table Tool

Parts of the Poster	Points	Attributes
Title	3–5	▪ Concise ▪ Interesting ▪ Fits the project
Pictures or Graphics	25	▪ Appropriate ▪ Clear ▪ Easy to understand ▪ Bold ▪ Colorful ▪ Gets the message across

I am convinced that more students would turn in quality work if they knew what that was. A rubric or matrix is a great way to let students know what we expect. The fastest and clearest way to create these is by using a computer. A simple matrix or rubric can be made by using the table tool in most word-processing programs. Great Websites for learning to create rubrics include www.rubricator.com and www.rubrics. com.

Table 2.2 is a simple rubric created using the table tool in a word-processing program. Table 2.3 is a simple matrix created with the same tool.

3

Using Media for Teaching

Through each time period in history, education has made an effort to reach the needs of the students of the time by using teaching methods that are familiar to them. For the generation of World War II, that teaching method was primarily auditory. After all, that generation listened to the radio, listened to each other, and read books for pleasure. The media of that time is not the same media of this generation. Today's students are born into a world of visual, auditory, and kinesthetic experiences. It would be unproductive to try to teach them using only the methods and media from the World War II era.

Our students are well versed in using various auditory, visual, and kinesthetic hardware and software in most aspects of their lives. In this chapter, we will examine the expectations for our students in regard to technology as well as ways to enhance learning using various forms of media, especially the computer.

THE BASICS

Whether your school uses national standards for educational computing, such as the National Educational Technology Standards (NETS), a state program, or have designed your own standards, there are some common threads that all standards should contain. Here is a breakdown of those expectations based on the five threads provided by the NETS project (www.cnets.iste.org):

1. Students should demonstrate that they have an understanding of the basic operations and concepts of technology. The demonstration of this standard varies by age and grade level of the students but, at a minimum, we should expect the following:
   - By the end of Grade 2, students can use input devices, such as the mouse, keyboard, and remote control, and output devices, such as the monitor and printer, to operate computers. They should be able to use appropriate technology resources in their learning.
   - By the end of Grade 5, students can use a keyboard and other common input and output devices. They can also understand the use of technology in daily life.
   - By Grade 8, students understand the concepts underlying hardware, software, connectivity, and the practical applications to learning and problem solving. They can also identify and solve routine hardware and software problems.
   - By Grade 12, students can make informed choices in regard to which system, resources, and services to use for each project.

2. Students should understand the social, ethical, and human issues related to technology and should practice responsibility in the use of technology systems, information, and software.
   - By the end of Grade 2, students can use the appropriate terminology when working with technology. They can also demonstrate appropriate ethical behaviors when using technology.
   - By the end of Grade 5, students should be able to discuss the ethics of using technology, including the consequences of inappropriate use.

- By the end of Grade 8, students should exhibit an understanding of the ethics of computer use and should be able to discuss the topic in class.
- By the end of Grade 12, students can demonstrate and promote the legal and ethical behaviors among peers family and community regarding the use of technology.

3. Students should be able to use developmentally appropriate technology productivity tools.
   - By the end of Grade 2, students can create appropriate multimedia products with support from others.
   - By the end of Grade 5, students should be able to use the productivity tools, multimedia authoring, presentation, Web tools, digital cameras, and scanners for writing, communicating, and publishing.
   - By the end of Grade 8, students will be able to use such productivity tools as environmental probes, graphing calculators, exploratory environments, and Web tools.
   - By the end of Grade 12, students can make good decisions about using technology tools and resources for managing and communicating personal or professional information. Some of these uses include for finances, schedules, addresses, purchases, and correspondence. Students should also understand the real-world application of using these tools.

4. Students should be able to use developmentally appropriate technology communications tools.
   - By the end of Grade 2, students can use technology resources, puzzles, logical thinking programs, writing tools, digital cameras, and drawing tools to illustrate their ideas.
   - By the end of Grade 5, students should be able to use online resources, such as e-mail, online discussions, and Web environments, to participate in collaborative projects.

- By the end of Grade 8, students can design, develop, publish, and use various communication tools to enhance their classroom learning. They can also collaborate in small group situations to produce tools for use inside and outside the classroom.
- By the end of Grade 12, students can use online resources to meet the needs for collaboration, publications, communications, and productivity. They can also collaborate with peers on the use of these tools.

5. Students should be able to use developmentally appropriate research tools.
   - By the end of Grade 2, students can gather information and communicate using telecommunications with support from others.
   - By the end of Grade 5, students should be able to use telecommunications efficiently enough to access remote information for independent learning.
   - By the end of Grade 8, students can use technology resources, such as Web pages and videotapes, to demonstrate and communicate curriculum concepts to others.
   - By the end of Grade 12, students can use online resources appropriately for research on a variety of topics. They can use expert systems, intelligent agents, and simulations of real-world situations.

6. Students should be able to use developmentally appropriate problem-solving and decision-making tools.
   - By the end of Grade 2, students can use some technology tools for decision making and problem solving.
   - By the end of Grade 5, students can select the appropriate tools for problem solving and decision making.
   - By the end of Grade 8, students should understand the practical applications of technology to solve problems and to make decisions. They can also evaluate the appropriateness of these resources for real-world application.

- By the end of Grade 12, students can select and apply the online resources necessary for decision making and problem solving. They also know how to compile and disseminate information appropriately.

USING TECHNOLOGY
TO TEACH TO STANDARDS

In their new materials on the teaching strategies that make the most difference in student learning, Marzano, Norford, Paynter, Pickering, and Gaddy (2001) list various strategies that have a high effect on student learning based on the meta-analysis of research conducted under the auspices of the Mid-continent Regional Educational Laboratory. In addition to listing the strategies, they explain how to use them and provide the effect size (i.e., the percentage gain that can be expected when these strategies are used with students) for these strategies. The following strategies are provided from this body of research along with information on how the use of various media can facilitate the process. For the purposes of this book, I will take five of the strategies outlined by Marzano, Norford et al. (2001) and explain the role of technology in their facilitation.

Using Nonlinguistic
Representations of the Learning

One of the most powerful learning tools in terms of student achievement is the use of nonlinguistic organizers. According to Marzano, Norford et al. (2001), using nonlinguistic organizers appropriately in the classroom can raise the learning level of students from the 50th percentile to the 77th percentile. Nonlinguistic organizers rely on their structure rather than a lot of words to convey meaning. Since at least 87% of the students in any given classroom are visual learners (i.e., they learn better when they can see the learning), using these tools is critical to meeting the needs of today's learners.

Several Websites are available to help students create various types of organizers, depending on the purpose. The sites include www.inspiration.com, which has hundreds of ideas for creating everything from mind maps to chains to your own creations. A second Website that I like very much is www.thinkingmaps.com, which provides a variety of structures to help students create personal meaning for the learning.

Understanding Similarities and Differences

Marzano, Norford et al. (2001) include comparing, classifying, creating metaphors, and creating analogies as the processes involved in understanding similarities and differences. The authors contend that "research tells us that students need explicit structure when they first begin identifying similarities and differences. Research also shows that graphic and symbolic representations can help students to understand and effectively use processes for identifying similarities and differences." According to these authors, the use of strategies to teach students to compare and contrast can move a student from the 50th percentile to the 95th percentile in terms of understanding. Graphic and symbolic representations of the learning are wonderful tools for teaching these concepts to students.

Let's look at ways that various media can help in the study of similarities and differences. First, teachers can learn a great deal about how to create nonlinguistic or graphic organizers for learning by using such Websites as www.thinkingmaps.com or www.inspiration.com.

In order for students to understand similarities and differences, they must understand the concept of *attributes*, which are the qualities that make something what it is. For example, the attributes of a bicycle are handlebars, wheels, seat, fender, gears, chain, and so forth.

I might begin a lesson by using a graphic model called an *attribute wheel* to teach attributes. Figure 3.1 is an example of an attribute wheel. Each spoke should contain an attribute of

Figure 3.1   Attribute Wheel

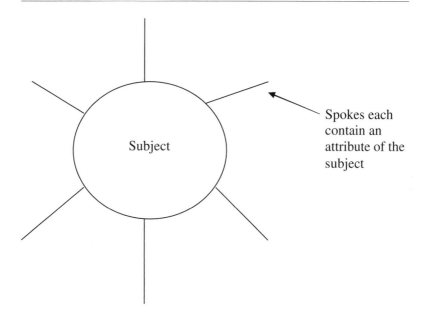

Spokes each
contain an
attribute of the
subject

the person, place, or thing that is being analyzed. When comparing two or more things, an attribute wheel is made for each. For example, we are going to compare a noun and a pronoun so I will need an attribute wheel for each.

Next, I can use a linguistic chart to provide information about the noun and pronoun from the attribute wheel in terms of how they are alike and how they are different. I can use the information that has been created in my chart to create a Venn diagram, placing the information from the right of my chart on the right side of my Venn diagram and the information from the left side of my chart on the left side of my diagram. The information in the center of the chart goes in the center of the diagram. Many students have trouble with Venn diagrams. By teaching them to do a compare and contrast chart first, we make Venn diagrams easier to design. Not only are all of these organizers (attribute wheels, charts, Venn diagrams) created by computer, but the directions and tools for creating them is available online.

More and more, we see the need for students to be able to compare and contrast items on high-stakes tests. Next time you examine the benchmarks for your grade level or subject area, look at how many times students must be able to identify attributes and know how two or more things are alike and how they are different.

Using Advance Organizers

Advance organizers provide a concrete way for students to organize information so that they can review, sort, and study it more effectively. Again, the Internet is full of ideas for advance organizers. According to Marzano, Norford et al. (2001), using advance organizers to help prepare students for new learning can move students up 22 percentile points.

I have provided an example of an advance organizer for keeping up with math formulas in Table 3.1. Other examples of advance organizers are journals, outlines, and graphic models. Interactive notebooks are a great way for students to make sense of the information. In these notebooks, students actively respond to information by recording class and reading notes on the right side and processing notes and graphics on the left side. Suggestions for processing notes include personal reactions, summaries, cartoons, graphic maps, poems, metaphors, and illustrations. An example of an interactive notebook is provided in Figure 3.2.

Specifically Teaching Vocabulary

When we teach vocabulary up front, before the lesson, we are more assured that students will be successful. It makes sense that, if students understand the terminology involved in the learning, they will be more apt to understand the learning. If you want to raise test scores, specifically teach the vocabulary of the test as well. Marzano, Norford et al. (2001) say that the best way to teach vocabulary is to provide opportunities

Table 3.1   A Linguistic Organizer for Mathematics

Formula or Principle	Terms Used With the Formula/ Principle	Purpose of the Formula/ Principle	Mathematical Expression	Other Information
Adding fractions	Denominator Numerator Common factors	Adding and multiplying fractions correctly	$1/5 \times 1/5$	If the denominators are the same, add the numerators, then use the sum as the numerator of the answer and the common denominator as the denominator of the answer. If the denominators have a common factor, multiply the common factors and other factors to find a common denominator. If the denominators do not have common factors, multiply the denominators and use the product as a common denominator, and then convert the items to equivalent fractions with common denominators by multiplying the numerator and denominator of each fraction by the same number.

for students to create mental models of the words. In Table 3.2, I have provided an example of how this might be done using graphics from the Internet.

Figure 3.2   Interactive Notebooks

In these notebooks, students actively respond to information by recording class and reading notes on the right side and processing notes and graphics on the left side.

Suggestions for left-side processing include personal reactions, summaries, cartoons, graphic maps, poems, metaphors, illustrations, etc.

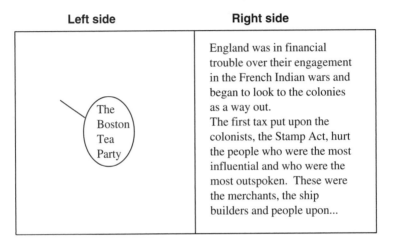

Building Connections Up Front

One of the most powerful tools for helping students understand from the beginning is accessing prior knowledge at the beginning of a new unit of study. This means that we find out what our students already know about the learning and, if they do not know anything, we produce an experience to help them make a connection. For example, prior to a study of the Romantic Period in literature, a teacher might ask students to define their ideal romantic hero or heroine. Secondary students have no trouble doing that, since they are very emotionally involved with love and romance at this age.

However, if the new unit of study is on world hunger, most of our students won't have prior knowledge: They are not hungry because they have food. They may be on diets

Table 3.2   Using Graphics to Clarify Vocabulary

Vocabulary Word	Definition	Graphic Example
Amphibian	Amphibians are vertebrates that are cold blooded and hatched from eggs.	

or have used their lunch money for something else, but most do not know real hunger as it is known throughout the world. I might begin a unit on world hunger by showing pictures from the Internet of the world's hungry so that I build a connection for them about what it looks like. A great source for such pictures is www.pbs.org.

HIGHER-LEVEL THINKING SKILLS

More and more, students are being required to prove their ability to use higher-level thinking in the products they create and on standardized tests. While it is still difficult to create assessment instruments that allow us to analyze our students' thinking abilities beyond knowledge, comprehension, and application, great progress has been made.

Let's identify the higher-level thinking skills most often discussed in the literature and how technology can create a bridge to these golden nuggets.

Thinking Skills That Demonstrate Understanding

Analyzing ideas. Help students understand mathematics with such sites as www.mathforum.org, where they can ask Dr. Math those perplexing questions. At the CNN students' news agency (www5.cnn.com/fyi/), students can get current on current events. The information is set in such categories as world events, business/mathematics, and health.

Compare and contrast. This skill is showing up more and more on high-stakes tests and is more complicated to learn than it might seem. In order to understand how things are alike and different, students must understand the meaning of attributes and they must be able to identify which attributes are important. For example, a student might be writing an essay about two people from history and may use their birthplace as an attribute to show how they are different. That attribute is important if the birthplace made a major difference in their lives, but if their birthplaces are similar, that attribute is not significant. Use the Website www.thinkingmaps.com for teaching attributes and how to make compare-and-contrast charts, or make your own using the chart tool in your word-processing program.

Classification/Definition. At www.lii.org, students can find information on a variety of topics by category, such as social issues, people and computers, science, and technology. Your students can also be a part of the Theban Mapping Project in Cairo (www.thebanmappingproject.com), which is working to prepare a comprehensive archaeological database of Thebes. The site includes an interactive atlas of tomb mappings, more than 250 detailed maps, and 66 narrated tours of the valley's corridors and chambers.

Creative Thinking That Leads to an Original Product

It has been said that we are all creative until the third grade and then our creativity takes a nosedive. Why the third grade? Maybe it is the volume of information that we have to tackle by that time. After all, students are heavily being tested by that time, and testing is serious business. Whatever the reason, the good news is that we can relearn to be creative. Generally, the steps to creative thinking are as follow:

1. Being able to generate many ideas or possibilities. Brainstorming is one of the tools used to teach students

to do this. When students are researching a subject, they brainstorm by searching the Internet for possible sites that might be of help to them. Running search engines is a way of brainstorming today.

2. Once students have many ideas on the table, they have to make choices about which tools to use. The second part of creative thinking is generating alternative possibilities. Once students know about sources, including what constitutes a primary and a secondary source, they can begin to make good choices. For primary resources, try taking your students to the Museum of Modern art at www.moma.org and view their database of information.

Creative thinking also means that students will come up with new ideas or be able to combine ideas to come up with their own. (Remember analysis and synthesis from Bloom's Taxonomy.) Furthermore, creative thinking means being able to design or understand analogies and metaphors and to associate one thing with another. We have discussed this aspect as we talked about compare-and-contrast as a thinking skill in the previous section.

Critical Thinking That Leads to the Ability to Make Judgments

Critical thinking is the ability to examine and break apart information so that decisions and judgments can be made. The steps in critical thinking to make judgments include the following:

- *Assessing basic information*—Explicitly teach students the difference in primary and secondary resources and where each is appropriate.
- *Accuracy of observation/reliability of sources*—Try the encyclopedia of folklore, myth, and legend at www. encyclopediamythica.com to help your students identify and distinguish fact from fiction.

- *Assessing inferences, use of evidence*—Follow one school that incorporated Fridays and crime scene investigation into Forensic Friday: CCSI—Classroom Crime Scene Investigation—at www.enc.org. This innovative science teacher creates a crime scene each week through which his students must work to determine the perpetrator of the crime. Teachers in the building eagerly volunteer to be the guilty party each week. Students can only solve the crime through the evidence.
- *Casual explanation/prediction*—If you would like to start your own crime scene unit, a good place to begin is www.forensicdna.com.
- *Generalization*—The International Monetary Fund's website (www.imf.org) to search for the online Monetary Mania, use www.monetarymania.com, which is designed as a quiz show to discover your knowledge level on money.
- *Conditional reasoning/categorical reasoning*—If you want your students to not only read about conditional reasoning but to see it, a great Website is www.physics.nad. ru/Physics/English, where students can view the ten "most beautiful" experiments. For example, the site features Galileo, who dared to question Greek scholars—including Aristotle, who said that heavy objects fall faster than light ones. In the 1500s, challenging this belief was unthinkable. Galileo is said to have dropped two different weights from Pisa's leaning tower to prove that they would land at the same time. Students can see the experiment for themselves at this Website.

Bloom's Taxonomy

A study of higher-level thinking would not be complete without looking at Benjamin Bloom's (1956) taxonomy of thinking skills. Bloom's Taxonomy categorizes learning that involves intellectual capabilities.

Working with technology can help students to reach the higher levels of Bloom's Taxonomy, especially analysis, synthesis, and evaluation. For example, let's say that a classroom teacher wants her students to be able to

- Understand scientific investigation and the importance of being accurate
- Gather information and to break it down for analysis
- Be able to create their own theories and ideas about the information, develop a hypothesis, and then evaluate the hypothesis after the experiments and data have been collected

The teacher might design a unit like the Forensic Friday one mentioned above. Some Websites that the teacher might use to assist the students as they look at the forensic evidence include the following:

- www.cbs.com/primetime/csi: This is the official Website of the program *CSI: Crime Scene Investigation*, and it's a good site to help the teacher prepare cases for her students to examine.
- www.crime-scene-investigator.net/index.html. This site offers information as well as a link to many other sites about crime scene investigation.
- www.schoolnet.ca. This Website offers lessons for students, including the how-to on DNA fingerprinting, chromatography, soil analysis, and much more.
- www.fbi.gov. This is the official FBI Website for kids who want to learn about crime scene investigations. Students can follow actual crime evidence as it goes through the FBI lab. The site includes a special agent challenge that changes each month.

In this unit of study, students are actively involved in the learning, and they are learning at a high level—painlessly.

4

Using Media
to Enhance
Student
Products

I n Chapter 2, I said that procedural knowledge demonstrates
to us what students can do with the declarative information
that they have learned. Processes are an integral part of teaching and learning. If memorizing facts were all we did in school,
we would have a very watered-down, minimal view of learning. Before students demonstrate to us what they know through
processes and products, they need some specific and direct
teaching on how to conduct the process. For example, nonlinguistic organizers are a great tool for learning, but if students
have not been taught how to create them or when to use them,
they are of little use. Students must explicitly be taught how to
create organizers. In addition, they must be given sufficient
time to shape them into their own creation and to practice so
that making them becomes automatic.

When placing students into research for independent
projects, some specific rules should be laid out so that the

students are more likely to be successful and to create a quality product. In the time before I discovered this information, I would assign my students to come up with an idea for a product based on something we had studied, and I would challenge them to do the work at a quality level. I discovered two things very quickly: First, what I considered to be quality and what my students considered to be quality were not the same thing, and, second, my gifted students were not really being challenged, because they could slop together something to turn in knowing that it would be better than anything turned in by the regular students.

When I began to use the information that I am about to share with you, two things happened: My regular education students began to create some exciting and wonderful quality products, and my gifted students were challenged as never before, because sloppy work no longer was accepted.

Here are the steps to eliciting a quality product.

MAKING CHOICES ON PRODUCTS

At a beginning level, I do not allow my students to invent their own projects. I have found that, until they have done some successful projects, they need to be provided with many ideas from which to choose. I do not assign independent projects until my students have been in my classroom long enough for me to have a clear idea about where they are in regard to abilities. On the other hand, I do not want my students to work on projects that are at a much lower level than they are capable. Using Bloom's Taxonomy as a guide, I decide the lowest level on which they can work: They can always work at a higher level but not at a lower one.

I provide a variety of projects for each level of Bloom's Taxonomy. Many of my ideas for projects come from Joyce Jontune's Website, www.engine-uity.com. Her ideas are for kindergarten through college age students and are of a high level. A word of caution here: Her projects were designed for gifted programs, so a third-grade project idea is for gifted third graders.

Here is the way project ideas might look at each level of Bloom's Taxonomy.

Knowledge Level

The knowledge level of Bloom's Taxonomy deals with information gathering and is the lowest level for projects. Student projects at this level would teach students how to gather research. Projects at this level may also be used before moving your students into more sophisticated research. You may want to show them how to find quality research on the Internet and how to know the difference between a primary and a secondary source. Primary source materials are materials that were written at the time of the event and include the following:

- Diaries, letters, and e-mails
- Speeches, testimony, and interviews
- Newspaper articles or news film or video
- Autobiographies
- Statistics and raw data sets
- Original scientific research
- Legislative hearings and bills
- Pictures and maps
- Poetry, drama, novels, music, and art
- Artifacts, such as jewelry, tombstones, furniture, and clothing

Some Websites that provide original material include the following:

- www.newsbank.com—A commercial company that charges for its services
- www.gettysbug.edu/library—This site offers access to early American documents.
- http://odur.let.rug.nl/—This is the "From Revolution to Reconstruction" site that includes primary source materials from the *Magna Carta* to Martin Luther King, Jr.'s "I have a dream" speech.

- www.ibiblio.org/expo/deadsea.scrolls.exhibit/intro. html—This Website includes information on and pictures of the Dead Sea Scroll
- www.yale.edu/lawweb—This site includes law and history documents
- www.memory.loc.gov/ammem/ammemhome.html— This is a government resource for primary materials
- http://personal.pitnet.net/primarysources—This site has an extensive list of other sites for primary sources.
- www.historynet.com—This site offers access to historical documents.
- www.teachersfirst.com—A free Website for teachers.

If you want help with ideas for using these documents in the classroom, the Teaching With Documents Website (www.edteck.com/dbq/) is there to help. Another site that provides many ideas for using primary resources is www. memory.loc.gov/ammem/ndlpedu/lessons/primary.html.

What, then, do we mean by *secondary sources*? The following are examples of secondary documents (i.e., those written by people who were not eyewitnesses or written after the time period of the event):

- Encyclopedias
- Literature reviews or literary criticism
- Many magazine articles
- Journal articles that are not primary reports of new research
- Reviews of books, movies, music, and plays
- A book written in 1995 about the causes of the French Revolution

At the knowledge level, I use a matrix that requires my students to tell me where they got the research and whether it is a primary or secondary source. Table 4.1 is an example of a matrix that I designed for a unit on immigration using the table tool on my word processor. I have divided the reasons into categories for the students to research. The columns

Table 4.1   Sample Matrix for Research

Reasons Why People Immigrate

Political	P/S	Social	P/S	Religious	P/S	Economic	P/S

labeled *P/S* are for students to indicate to me whether the resource is a primary or a secondary resource.

Here are some ideas for knowledge-level projects your students can do:

- Write an ad for a city of their choice to convince people to come there for vacation.
- Make a card file of facts about alligators that includes at least 25 facts.
- Create a newspaper story using *what, who, when,* and *where.*
- Draw and label the parts of something.
- Make a circle map of something.

Comprehension Level

At the comprehension level, students not only gather information, they demonstrate that they understand what they gather. For example, in a knowledge-based project, students put together a fact file on alligators. The act of gathering the facts, however, does not mean that they understand those facts. At the comprehension level, students would go a step further by summarizing the information into a short essay.

Some ideas for a comprehension-level project include asking students to:

- Gather information on the digestive system and draw a tree map using tools from the Internet to group the various parts of the system.
- Arrange given information from the least important to the most important. Use a graphic model, such as a flowchart diagram, to show the information.
- Show space-time relationships or part-whole relationships.
- Create a flow map on the sequence of an event.

Application Level

At the application level, students are able to gather data, understand what they have gathered, and then to do something with the data beyond just simple rote memorization. For example, the student who gathered facts on alligators and summarized the information might, in an application-level project, put together a manual using a publishing tool on how to hunt for alligators.

For an application-level project, you might have your students:

- Gather information on the various math concepts studied in your grade level, place them in categories, and create a linguistic organizer, such as a spreadsheet or table, for this information so that it could be used by a new student in the class. Use the Bubble Map or Flow Map from www.thinkingmaps.com for your project.
- Compare and contrast tornados and hurricanes using a Double Bubble Map or other graphic organizer and then draw conclusions from the data. Use the Double Bubble Map from www.thinkingmaps.com.
- Gather data on the characteristics of the major leaders of the world; design a matrix using a word-processing table tool or using graphics software with the leaders listed on one side and the characteristics across the top; and then, from this information, write a persuasive letter to a would-be leader explaining the important points in becoming a world leader.

Analysis Level

With the analysis level, we are finally into higher-order thinking. Students at this level are able to analyze data and draw important conclusions from it. They can make a plan and follow it through based on the data provided.

Examples of projects at this level include asking students to:

- Gather and chart data on a given topic; draw conclusions based on that data; and present the data in some way, such as in a news article, letter to the editor, manual, guide, or spreadsheet. Use the computer's productivity tools, such as the tools for drawing, for setting up a table or chart, for creating graphics, or for capturing sound, or use software that provides templates for news articles, manuals, and so forth, to do so.
- Study the information available on gnomes and hypothesize in a letter to the editor what will happen if. . . .
- Gather information on terrorist activities and prepare a manual on what to do if. . . .
- Look for patterns in data and plot them in a spreadsheet program, such as Microsoft Excel.

Synthesis Level

The synthesis level is a high level of thinking reserved primarily in the past for gifted students. Regular education students, however, are quite capable of working at this creative level if shown the way. Synthesis involves taking something apart and putting it back together in new and unusual ways or inventing something new.

Some examples of projects at this level include having students:

- Create a way to help other students learn vocabulary so that they will not forget it. Students can use presentation software, such as PowerPoint, to teach the vocabulary to their fellow students.

- Invent a new type of soda and present the new product to the class. Students can use a graphics program to present their new product.
- Design a solution to prove, show, or improve something. Students can then prepare a brochure using productivity tools available on the computer.

Evaluation Level

The evaluation level is considered to be the highest level of thinking, because, in order to evaluate, one must be able to know, understand, apply, analyze, and synthesize.

Student projects at this level might include:

- Writing a letter to the editor evaluating something
- Demonstrating, by using evaluation and decision-making matrices, how they reached their conclusion about a subject
- Convincing their fellow students about an argument through a PowerPoint presentation

FOLLOWING A GUIDE FOR RESEARCH

After making choices about the project level and product, the next step is to provide students with a guide or matrix for doing research. Table 4.2 shows part of a matrix that I created using the table tool in my word processing program and that I use for a project in which students give a speech. There are certainly many ways to do this, but the point is not to leave this step to chance. I also give my students a matrix or rubric at this point to show them exactly what I mean by quality. Give it to them before they start their project so that they know what is expected from the beginning and so that there are no "gotchas" in the evaluation.

By using this matrix, students know my expectation. There is no question what should be contained in a persuasive letter and which attributes make the letter of high quality.

Table 4.2   Sample Evaluation Matrix

Essential Parts of a Speech	Points Earned [Proved by the teacher after the speech]	Attributes That Make the Speech a Quality Product
Body language		■ Good posture ■ Shows confidence ■ Makes eye contact with audience ■ Uses appropriate gestures
Introduction		■ Attention grabbing ■ Captures the interest of the audience
Projection of voice		■ Clarity ■ Pronunciation ■ Strong ■ Appropriate volume
Presenter added variety by . . .		■ Varying pace ■ Varying volume ■ Creating visual imagery ■ Using vivid language ■ Using supporting details
Ending		■ Strong ■ Related back to the theme or opening sentence

There is no "gotcha" in the grading: Either the attributes are there or they are not. Since some of the parts of the letter have a higher point value than others, I usually provide the possible point value as well. That way, if students wait until the last minute to complete the project, they at least know what kinds

Form 4.1   Sample Contract for a Project

Student Project Planner

Student _____ Teacher _____

Topic_____

Initial research to be completed by: _____

Preliminary product outlines/Designs to be completed by:

_____

Finished products to be presented on: _____

Product will be presented in the following formats: _____

_____

_____

_____

Members of the team: _____

_____

Signed (Students)   Teacher

of points they are losing by eliminating attributes. Another advantage to using this kind of matrix for student projects is that it provides documentation of the student's work. If a parent or student questions the grade, there is concrete evidence about how the grade was calculated. The feedback is also specific, because it is given in terms of attributes of quality. By giving students accurate and specific feedback, we can raise their level of understanding considerably.

Also at this stage of a project, provide your students with a guide for planning and dialogue during the project. I ask my students to contract with me for what they are doing. Not only is this an example of what they might be asked to do in the real world, it solidifies for my students the importance of planning and staying on task. Form 4.1 is an example of a contract that might be used.

At the end of the project, I go back to the rubric or matrix that was given at the beginning to the project for assessing the student's work. By using this method, there are fewer chances for surprises from me or from my students, and the quality of the work has become phenomenal.

How does the use of media make the work of student projects more productive? Certainly we have been assigning research to our students for many years prior to the use of media in the classroom. Sometimes the resulting work was satisfactory; sometimes it was not. Using media adds depth to the projects and products that our students complete, and it helps us to work smarter instead of just harder.

5

Viewing the Big Picture

Keeping Up

Websites and technology change daily and, while writing this book, I was aware that many of the Websites I was writing about might not be around in the coming years. I want this book to be a relevant guide for several years to come, so this chapter provides Websites that I think are most likely to have e-longevity. These are sites of organizations and groups that can keep you up to date on the best Web information available in any given year. The sites and a brief description of the organization associated with it follow.

- www.mcrel.org—The Mid-continent Regional Education Laboratory (McREL) specializes in research on what works in education. They have been at the forefront of the research on standards and have helped write the standards in some states. Researchers Robert Marzano and Debra Pickering author many books and articles for the McREL. At the time of this writing, Robert Marzano has more than 20 books on the market. You can run a search on this Website by topic to get a list of resources.

- www.ncrel.org—The North Central Regional Education Laboratory (NCREL) is strong in the field of computer technology. The Library in the Sky section of the NCREL site has a feature called "Pick of the Week," which lists several outstanding Websites each week. In addition, you can access previous "Pick of the Week" lists. For example, a recent week brought up Quiz Hub, which the NCREL site describes as

  > a center for online learning activities [whose] topic areas include biology, chemistry, English, geography, history, French, German, Spanish and college prep. [The site] helps students memorize chemical elements, world capitals, historical dates, U.S. presidents, French, German, Spanish, SAT vocabulary, etc.

- As a matter of fact, any of the regional education laboratories throughout the United States are great sources for you. You can locate them by doing a search for "regional education laboratory" in any of the major Internet search engines.

- www.ascd.org—The Association for Supervisors and Curriculum Developers (ASCD) has a well-respected Website with information on just about any topic in education.

- www.nassp.org—The National Association for Secondary School Principals (NASSP). This organization promotes policies and tools for secondary schools. Secondary teachers will get many ideas from this site for their classroom and will be kept up to date on "hot topics" in education.

- www.naesp.org—The National Association for Elementary School Principals (NAESP). The NAESP site is dedicated to what works best for elementary school students and staff. Elementary school teachers will find good ideas for the classroom and for the whole school.

- www.lii.org—The librarians' index to the Internet is a valuable resource written by categories of information.

- www.netc.org—This national computer technology Website has great ideas for using computers in the classroom, especially for student projects. Recently, they added a section called Classrooms at Work that provides in-depth project ideas written and used by teachers. This part of the Website can be accessed at www.netc.org/classroom@work.

- www.nmsa.org—The National Middle School Association (NMSA) provides information for teachers and students at the middle school level.

- www.us.gov—This government Website provides a wealth of links to sites for use by schools.

- www.multi-intell.com—This site leads you to information about using multiple intelligences information in the classroom.

- www.encyclopediamythica.com—A good encyclopedia site of myth and folklore.

If you want to know all the bells and whistles, I suggest you look into these Websites:

- www.thecommittedsardine.net—Ian Jukes and Bruce McDonald manage this wonderful site, which has the latest and newest information on technology.

- www.nctp.com—The National Center for Technology Planning (NCTP) contains technology plans, articles, and much more.

- www.cnets.iste.org—This site provides national standards in technology.

- www.iste.org—The International Society for Technology in Education (ISTE) Website provides a good example of the kinds of technology standards, by grade level, that should be employed in every school.

- www.ed.gov/technology/elearning—This is the Website for the Government Office for Educational Technology. Through it, teachers have an opportunity to look at standards for their grade level and ideas for implementation.

- www.nea.org—The National Education Association (NEA) is committed to helping all students succeed and provides ideas for the classroom as well as suggested Websites for teachers.
- www.nsba—The National School Boards Association (NSBA) is the organization for school board members and superintendents. This site deals with national issues, such as violence in schools.

BEING AN AGENT OF CHANGE

Once you begin to put into place the ideas from this book, you will probably have questions from your fellow teachers about using new ideas in the classroom. The best way to become an agent of change in any given context is to begin with people where they are. If your school is just beginning to use technology, start with a few of the ideas that have worked for you and build from there. Many schools trying to change move so quickly that the staff is left gasping for air.

Begin with people (and students) where they are, and move them to where they need to be using a step-by-step process. When people at my school began using some of these ideas in our classrooms, we went through 15 days of training on teaching methods, climate, tools, and so forth. Now, you don't need 15 days of training, but you need to use a few things, become comfortable with them, and then add to them. A good beginning place is to use linguistic and nonlinguistic organizers, since research shows that they have a powerful impact on student learning.

CREATING A PLAN
FOR THE CLASSROOM

As you create a plan for using technology in your classroom, use Table 5.1 as a guide. The table is based on the standards

Table 5.1   Guide for Using Technology in the Classroom

Student	Word-Processing Program	Spreadsheet Program	Graphics Tools	Publishing	Web Master	Internet Program
Anderson	M	I	M			
Azure	I	M	M			

listed in Chapter 1, and I created it using the table tool in my word-processing program.

I also use my computer to track my students' ability to use various tools. For example, when my student named Anderson shows mastery of the word-processing productivity tool (*Word-Processing Program*), I place an M in that space by his name. He is at an introductory level for using a spreadsheet program, so I have placed an I in the appropriate space. When he demonstrates mastery, I will replace the I with an M. If there is no mark in the space, it means that the student has not been introduced to the tool as yet.

TECHNOLOGY = SUCCESS

Using a variety of media in the classroom not only builds interest but also assures the classroom teacher that all modalities and interests are being served. It is the silver bullet to getting students to higher-order thinking without groans and moans. Technology levels the playing field for all students as no other single tool is able to do. The computer does not care if the student is male, female, rich, poor, Hispanic, Native American, or African American. Moreover, students today spend so much time on the Internet, and using computers in general, that teaching with technology is a natural way to reach these students. Interest rises, discipline problems decrease, and quality is paramount in a classroom that appropriately uses technology.

One of the main concerns about using computers in the classroom is the appropriateness of the computers to the standards and work provided. In this book, I hope that you have seen that computers not only enhance the work of the classroom, they also increase the probability that students will be successful.

Vocabulary Summary

I am providing a vocabulary summary for the information covered in this book. For a complete list of terms related to technology including new terms, try the Website www. webopedia.com.

Bloom's Taxonomy

Attributed to the work of Benjamin Bloom, this taxonomy of thinking skills is built on the idea that the basic thinking skill is knowledge, which means students know the information. The second level is comprehension, which means students understand the learning. The third level, application, means students are able to use the information. The fourth level, analysis, means students are able to break the learning down into manageable parts. The fifth level, synthesis, means students can take something apart and put it back together in new and unusual ways or can create something new. The highest level is evaluation, which means students are able to form judgments. It is important to note that the taxonomy is not built on difficulty. A project at the knowledge level can be difficult. The taxonomy is built on complexity of thought.

Channel One

Channel One is a media outlet that has been controversial from its inception. A television news service operated by Primedia broadcast daily in schools throughout the country, Channel

One contains approximately ten minutes of news and two minutes of commercials. The program is controversial because it provides commercialism to a "kept audience," since students are mandated to attend school.

Classroom Climate

Classroom climate refers to the feel of the room, which includes physical factors such as temperature, lighting, and seating, as well as the emotional climate, which includes the way that students and teachers relate to one another. Media can alter the climate in a classroom by eliciting strong emotions and by providing new ways for students to work together, as in the case of using e-mail to put together a project.

Classroom Management

Classroom management refers to the way in which a teacher organizes the class, administers routines, and handles behavior in a given classroom. Media has a profound effect on classroom management because it not only helps the teacher to plan better, but also provides graphic organizers for students. In addition, since students are used to and expect multimedia in their lives, the use of good media enhances student interest and cuts down on discipline problems.

Cognitive Development

Cognitive development is a process that begins at birth with learning through the senses and through observation. Media enhances that development.

Computer-Assisted Instruction

Educational programs that are delivered primarily through computers fall into the category of *computer-assisted instruction* (CAI). In this type of setting, teachers may explicitly teach principles and then place students into CAI, or the students may be in a CAI situation with teachers acting more as mentors or coaches than as imparters of knowledge.

Creative and Productive Thinking

Developed by Paul Torrance (1979), *creative and productive thinking* includes fluency (many ideas), flexibility (many different ideas), originality, and evaluation.

Critical Thinking

Critical thinking is defined as logical thinking based on fact or evidence. The ultimate goal is for students to be able to make critical judgments.

The aspects of critical thinking are

1. Assessing basic information through observation
2. Assessing inferences by using evidence to explain, predict, form analogies and generalizations
3. Assessing inferences through deduction and being able to give conditional reasoning and/or categorical reasoning

Cyber Schools

Cyber schools are learning institutions that provide instruction primarily by computer via the Internet.

Direct Instruction

In *direct instruction,* the teacher provides clear, step-by-step instruction on the information to be learned. This is in contrast to other teaching methods, such as discovery learning, computer-assisted instruction, or investigation.

Discovery Learning

Discovery learning is designed so that students discover facts and principles rather than having them explained by a textbook or a teacher.

Distance Learning

Distance learning provides opportunities for students to take classes through computers and the Internet at a location other than the traditional classroom.

Higher-Order Thinking

Resnick and Resnick (1997) define *higher-order thinking* as "the kind of thinking needed when the path to finding a solution is not specified, and yields multiple solutions." Examples of higher-order thinking include critical thinking, creative thinking, and the higher levels of Bloom's Taxonomy (i.e., analysis, synthesis, and evaluation).

Linguistic Organizers

Linguistic organizers (also known as advance organizers) are visual tools used to help students organize information in the classroom. They rely on words rather than pictures or symbols for the learning. An example of a linguistic organizer is a journal.

Multimedia

Multimedia refers to using more than one medium for communication. For example, using music, PowerPoint presentations, animation, and voice would be an example of using multimedia.

Nonlinguistic Organizer

A *nonlinguistic organizer* is a tool used to display information graphically in a concise format with a minimum of words. Because over 87% of learners are visual or kinesthetic, nonlinguistic organizers are an important way to help students organize information.

Primary Sources

In research, *primary sources* refers to information found originally as to where and who said it. For example, viewing a copy of the Declaration of Independence is not a primary source; the primary source would be the original document itself. We want students to know where the original information can be found.

Problem-Based Learning

Problem-based learning is a teaching technique that involves students in solving problems rather than the more conventional study of information. An example of a problem-based learning exercise is the Mega Olympus activity discussed in Chapter 1, in which students must determine the best Latin American country for the relocation of a corporation. Because the learning is in a real-world context, students are more apt to see the relevance of the learning.

Rubric

A *rubric* is a device used to measure the degree to which a student knows and understands the learning. Most rubrics have three to four levels of understanding, such as *novice, beginner, intermediate,* and *expert.* The rubric should list the characteristics of each level and should be given to students prior to any assignment for which grades will be taken. Rubrics can be computer generated, and some Internet sites provide tutorials for the teacher on designing effective rubrics.

Scaffolding

Scaffolding refers to the learning tools provided by a teacher to see that students are successful before placing them into independent learning. Teachers often provide a great deal of scaffolding at the beginning of a lesson, gradually decreasing the scaffolding as students become more independent in their learning.

Secondary Sources

Secondary sources in research are quotations or copies of original words and documents. Most of the information on the

Internet is secondary information and is usable as long as students know the original source. Some Websites, such as www.teacherfirst.com or www.law.emory.edu/FEDERAL/ conpict.html, provide samples of original documents. One of the original documents that I encountered when I visited a primary source facility was the original *New York Times* article after the sinking of the *Titanic* that says, "*Titanic* sinks, all aboard are safe." If I were doing research on the effect of the sinking of the ship on families back home, this information would be very significant: First, they hear that the ship is gone, then that their loved ones are safe—only to discover that they are dead.

Student Products

Student products are the end results of student learning. The products may be visual, auditory, or kinesthetic and should provide proof of student understanding of the factual knowledge. Student products are an example of procedural knowledge. This is sometimes referred to as *the project method* of teaching.

Vocabulary
Post-Test

At the beginning of this book, you were given a vocabulary list and a pre-test on that vocabulary. Below are the post-test and the answer key for the vocabulary assessment.

VOCABULARY POST-TEST

Instructions: For each question given, choose the best answer. Only one answer is correct.

1. Critics of technology use in schools have as their *main* concern . . .
   A. The research results on the use of technology in schools
   B. The inappropriate use of the Internet
   C. The appropriateness of the computer to the lessons
   D. The use of the computers by students to e-mail each other

2. In a classroom in which students are provided information in a step-by-step format, we say the students are being taught by . . .
   A. Discovery learning
   B. Problem-based learning
   C. Scaffolding
   D. Direct instruction

3. Students who rely on the Internet for research are primarily using what?
   A. Secondary sources
   B. Scaffolding
   C. Primary sources
   D. Problem-based learning

4. Marty Perez's language arts and social studies classes were given a newspaper article about a company that wants to relocate to a Latin American country. Ms. Perez has asked her students to work in small groups as they research and put together a proposal to sell the company on the country they have chosen. This type of teaching technique is called . . .
   A. Scaffolding
   B. Problem-based learning
   C. Primary sources
   D. Direct instruction

5. In Jim Brown's mathematics class, he uses music, PowerPoint, and discussion for teaching. What technique is Mr. Brown using?
   A. Problem-based learning
   B. Direct instruction
   C. Discovery learning
   D. Multimedia

6. Shonda Marshall is starting a unit on the Vietnam War. She has placed her students in small groups and given them a packet that contains maps of the area as it was at the time of the war, maps of the area as it is now, names of major battles, and the names of key players. Ms. Marshall took her class to the computer lab for a scavenger hunt to find the information required in her packet. What technique is Ms. Marshall using?
   A. Distance learning
   B. Discovery learning
   C. Primary sources
   D. Linguistic organizers

7. Which of the following statements is *not* true?
   A. Rubrics should be given to students prior to the learning.
   B. Rubrics show levels of understanding.
   C. Tutorials for rubrics are available on the Internet.
   D. Rubrics should not be used as an assessment for a unit of study.

8. Martina is a middle school student. Her teacher provides the students with a great deal of direct instruction and feedback at the beginning of a unit and then gradually puts the students into opportunities to learn on their own. Martina's teacher is practicing . . .
   A. Computer-assisted instruction
   B. Creative and productive thinking
   C. Scaffolding
   D. Problem-based learning

9. Students at Blair Elementary are working on a project that requires them to use forensic evidence to explain a given problem. Which of the following are the students *not* practicing?
   A. Problem-based learning
   B. Higher-order thinking
   C. Critical thinking
   D. Computer-assisted instruction

10. Nicole is taking a class on speech pathology on the Internet. This is an example of . . .
    A. Computer-assisted instruction
    B. Problem-based learning
    C. Distance learning
    D. Discovery learning

11. Which of the following would *not* be an example of a linguistic organizer?
    A. A mind map
    B. An outline
    C. A learning log
    D. A chart for math formulas

12. Which of the following would *not* be an example of a nonlinguistic organizer?
    A. A mind map
    B. A learning log
    C. A sequence organizer
    D. A fishbone

13. Using television as a media source sometimes draws criticism because . . .
    A. It is commercialized
    B. It takes up too much time
    C. It has questionable value
    D. It is too low tech

14. The modality most often found in school is . . .
    A. Multimodal
    B. Auditory
    C. Visual
    D. Kinesthetic

15. Students in Mr. Brown's class are using a Website that shows them the original Declaration of Independence. They are using . . .
    A. An expensive program
    B. Secondary sources
    C. Multimedia programming
    D. Primary sources

16. When teachers use the project method of teaching, they should remember that . . . (Which is *not* true?)
    A. They need procedural objectives
    B. They need examples from each modality
    C. Students do not need a lot of direction
    D. Students do need a lot of feedback

17. Kenny presented his report in PowerPoint. This is an example of . . .
    A. A visual product
    B. A kinesthetic product
    C. An auditory product
    D. A nonlinguistic product

18. Drew presented his report as a dialogue typed on the computer and read to the class. This is an example of . . .
    A. A visual product
    B. A kinesthetic product
    C. An auditory product
    D. A nonlinguistic product

19. Shelly presented her report as a model drawn on the computer accompanied by sound and motion. Her report is an example of . . .
    A. Multimedia
    B. A linguistic product
    C. Secondary sources
    D. Cyber schools

20. Margot created a computer game to help her fellow students learn math facts. This is an example of . . .
    A. Analysis
    B. Synthesis
    C. Evaluation
    D. Distance learning

Vocabulary Post-Test Answer Key

1. C		11. A	
2. D		12. B	
3. A		13. A	
4. B		14. C	
5. D		15. D	
6. B		16. C	
7. D		17. A	
8. C		18. C	
9. D		19. A	
10. C		20. B	

References

Bloom, B. S. (1956). *Taxonomy of educational objectives, Handbook I: Cognitive domain*. New York: McKay.

Garner, J. (1998). *We interrupt this broadcast*. Kansas City, MO: Andrews McMeel.

Jensen, E. (1997). *Completing the puzzle: The brain-compatible approach to learning* (2nd ed.). Del Mar, CA: The Brain Store.

Marzano, R. J. (2000). *Transforming classroom grading*. Alexandria, VA: Association for Supervision and Curriculum Development.

Marzano, R. J., Norford, J. S., Paynter, D. E., Pickering, D. J., & Gaddy, B. B. (2001). *A handbook for classroom instruction that works*. Alexandria, VA: Association for Supervision and Curriculum Development.

Marzano, R. J., Pickering, D. J., & Pollock, J. E. (2001). *Classroom instruction that works*. Alexandria, VA: Association for Supervision and Curriculum Development.

Resnick, O. P., & Resnick, L. B. (1997). The nature of literacy: An historical exploration. *Harvard Educational Review, 47*(3).

Tapscott, D. (1998). The net generation and the school. *The Milken Exchange on Education and Technology* (Online). Retrieved June 12, 2003, from www.milkenexchange.org/feature/tapscott_full. html.

Tileston, D. W. (2000). *Ten best teaching practices: How brain research, learning styles, and standards define teaching competencies*. Thousand Oaks, CA: Corwin Press.

Tileston, D. W. (2004a). *What every teacher should know about classroom management and discipline*. Thousand Oaks, CA: Corwin Press.

Tileston, D. W. (2004b). *What every teacher should know about instructional planning*. Thousand Oaks, CA: Corwin Press.

Tileston, D. W. (2004c). *What every teacher should know about learning, memory, and the brain*. Thousand Oaks, CA: Corwin Press.

Torrance, P. (1979). *Education and the creative potential*. Minneapolis: University of Minnesota Press.

Wenglinsky, H. (1998). *Does it compute?* Princeton, NJ: Educational Testing Service.

Index

Association for Supervisors and
    Curriculum Developers
    (ASCD), 52
Attribute wheel, 28-29,
    29 (figure)
Audio-visual presentations,
    18-19
Auditory learning, 3
Automaticity, 18, 20

Behavior management, 4-5
Bloom, B., 36
Bloom's Taxonomy, 36-37, 57
Brain-compatible learning, 2-3

Channel one, 57-58
Classroom climate, 58
Classroom management, 58
Cognitive development, 58
Computer-assisted instruction
    (CAI), 58-59
Contextualization, 4
Creative/productive thinking,
    34-35, 59
Critical thinking, 35-36, 59
Cyber schools, 59

Declarative objectives,
    12-13, 13 (figure)
    information, organization of, 16
    meaning construction, 13-15,
        14 (table)
    storage of information, 17
Direct instruction, 59
Discovery learning, 59
Distance learning, 60

Educational computing
    standards, 23-27
English language learners
    (ELLs), 4
Episodic memory system, 4
Equal opportunity, 2

Feedback specificity, 3, 5, 20

Gaddy, B. B., 27, 28, 30
Goal-setting, 13, 14 (table)
Government Office for
    Educational Technology, 53
Graphic organizers, 16
    attribute wheel, 28-29,
        29 (figure)
    interactive notebooks and,
        30, 32 (figure)
    mental models and, 18-19
    shaping information
        and, 20

Higher-order thinking skills, 60
    Bloom's Taxonomy of,
        36-37
    classification/definition, 34
    compare and contrast, 34
    creative thinking, original
        products and, 34-35
    critical thinking, decisions/
        judgments and, 35-36
    idea analysis, 33-34
    media resources and, 5-6
    standardized testing and, 33
    understanding, demonstration
        of, 33-34

Immersion, 20
Importance concept, 6
Impulsiveness, 13
Interactive notebooks, 30, 32 (figure)
Internalization of information,
    18, 20
International Society for
    Technology in Education
    (ISTE), 53
Internet resources:
    education organizations,
        Websites for, 51-54
    graphic organizers, 16, 17, 28, 30
    higher-order thinking skills
        and, 33-37
    learning, real-world applications
        and, 7
    lesson plan template, 9
    meaning construction and, 13-15
    mindjogs, 10-11
    project ideas, 40, 41-42, 53
    rubric development, 21
    state standards, 11
    storage tools, 17
Intrinsic motivation, 3-4

Jensen, E., 3, 16

Learning:
    brain-compatible learning, 2-3
    contextualization and, 4
    goal-setting and, 13, 14 (table)
    modalities for, 2, 3
    See also Lesson planning;
        Teaching process
Lesson planning:
    audio-visual presentations, 19
    declarative objectives, 12-17,
        13 (figure)
    matrix/rubric and, 20-21,
        21 (tables)
    meaning construction, 13-15,
        14 (table)
    mental models, construction
        of, 18-19
    mindjogs, 10-11
    organization of information, 16

procedural objectives,
    18-20, 28 (figure)
shaping information, 19-20
standards/benchmarks and, 11-12
steps in, 12 (figure)
storage of information, 17
templates for, 9
See also Teaching process
Linguistic organizers, 29, 60

Marzano, R. J., 6, 27, 28, 30
Mathematics learning, 5, 6, 31 (table)
Matrix, 20-21, 21 (table)
    evaluation matrix, 46-49,
        47 (table)
    research matrix, 42-43, 43 (table)
Meaning construction,
    13-15, 14 (table)
Media, 1-2
    behavior management and, 4-5
    brain-compatible learning
        and, 2-3
    higher-order thinking and, 5-6
    learning modalities and, 3
    memory function and, 4
    motivation and, 3-4
    real-world applications and, 6-7
    See also Teaching process;
        Technology
Memory:
    contextual learning and, 4
    episodic memory, 4
    semantic memory, 4
Mental models, 18-19,
    30-31, 33 (table)
Metacognitive system, 13
Mid-continent Regional
    Educational Laboratory
    (McREL), 27, 51
Mindjogs, 10-11
Mind mapping, 20
Modalities, 2, 3
Motivation:
    goal-setting and, 13
    media effects on, 3-4
    personal relevance and, 6-7
Multimedia, 5, 55, 60

National Association for
    Elementary School Principals
    (NAESP), 52
National Association for Secondary
    School Principals (NASSP), 52
National Center for Technology
    Planning (NCTP), 53
National Educational Technology
    Standards (NETS), 23-27
National Education Association
    (NEA), 54
National Middle School Association
    (NMSA), 53
National School Boards Association
    (NSBA), 54
Nonlinguistic organizers, 16, 17,
    27-28, 60
Norford, J. S., 27, 28, 30
The North Central Regional
    Education Laboratory
    (NCREL), 52

Organizational tools, 16, 17, 27-28, 30
Outcomes. *See* Student products

Pattern development, 16
Paynter, D. E., 27, 28, 30
Personal relevance, 6-7, 13
Pickering, D. J., 6, 27, 28, 30
Pollock, J. E., 6
Poverty:
    contextual learning and, 4
    personal relevance and, 6-7
PowerPoint presentations, 19, 60
Practice, 20
Primary sources, 41-42, 60-61
Problem-based learning, 61
Procedural objectives,
        18, 18 (figure)
    mental models, construction
        of, 18-19
    shaping information, 19-20
    See also Student products
Productive thinking,
    34-35, 59
Project method of teaching, 62
    See also Student products

Real-world applications, 2, 5, 6-7
Rehearsal, 20
Relevance, 6-7, 13
Resnick, L. B., 60
Resnick, O. P., 60
Rubrics, 2, 20-21, 21 (table), 61

Scaffolding, 61
Secondary sources, 42, 61-62
Self-system, 13
Semantic memory system, 4
Sensory input, 3
Shaping information, 19-20
Similarities/differences, 28-30
Standards, 3, 23-27
Storage of information, 17
Student products, 39-40, 62
    analysis-level projects, 45
    application-level projects, 44
    Bloom's Taxonomy and, 40-46
    comprehension-level projects,
        43-44
    contract sample for, 48 (form), 49
    creative thinking and, 34-35
    evaluation-level projects, 46
    knowledge-level projects, 41-43
    matrix development for, 42-43,
        43 (table), 46-49, 47 (table)
    primary sources and, 41-42
    secondary sources and, 42
    synthesis-level projects, 45-46

Tapscott, D., 3
Teaching process, 23
    advance organizers and, 30, 31
        (table), 32 (figure)
    attribute wheel, 28-29, 29 (figure)
    Bloom's Taxonomy and, 36-37
    educational computing
        standards and, 23-27
    higher-order thinking skills,
        33-37
    linguistic charts, 29
    nonlinguistic organizers
        and, 27-28
    prior knowledge, connections
        with, 32-33

project method and, 62
similarities/differences,
    understanding of, 28-30
strategies in, 27-33
vocabulary, mental modeling of,
    30-31, 33 (table)
See also Lesson planning;
    Student products
Technology, 2
    communications tools, 25-26
    developmental appropriateness
        and, 25-27
    educational computing
        standards, 23-27
    operations/concepts of, 24
    problem-solving/decision-
        making tools, 26-27
    productivity tools, 25
    research tools, 26
    social issues/ethics and, 24-25
    utilization of, 54-56, 55 (table)

Website resources, 51-54
    See also Media; Multimedia;
        Teaching process
Teenage Research Unlimited, 3
Torrence, P., 59

Understanding, 33-34

Visualization, 19
Visual learning, 3, 4, 5
    organizational tools, 16, 27-28
    PowerPoint presentations, 19, 60
Vocabulary:
    list of, xii
    post-test, 63-68
    pre-test, xiii-xvii
    summary of, 57-62

Web resources. *See* Internet
    resources
Wenglinsky, H., 6

**CORWIN
PRESS**

The Corwin Press logo—a raven striding across an open book—represents the happy union of courage and learning. We are a professional-level publisher of books and journals for K-12 educators, and we are committed to creating and providing resources that embody these qualities. Corwin's motto is "Success for All Learners."